21st Century
Junior Library

TALKING ABOUT
BODY IMAGE

Topics to Talk About

**AnneMarie McClain
and Lacey Hilliard**

Published in the United States of America by Cherry Lake Publishing Group
Ann Arbor, Michigan
www.cherrylakepublishing.com

Reading Adviser: Beth Walker Gambro, MS, Ed., Reading Consultant, Yorkville, IL
Book Designer: Jen Wahi

Library of Congress Cataloging-in-Publication Data

Names: Hilliard, Lacey, author. | McClain, AnneMarie, co-author.
Title: Talking about body image / written by Lacey Hilliard and AnneMarie McClain.
Description: Ann Arbor, Michigan : Cherry Lake Publishing, [2023] | Series: Topics to talk about | Includes bibliographical references and index. | Audience: Grades 2-3 | Summary: "How do we talk about body image? This book breaks down the topic of body image for young readers. Filled with engaging photos and captions, this series opens up opportunities for deeper thought and informed conversation. Guided exploration of topics in 21st Century Junior Library's signature style help readers to Look, Think, Ask Questions, Make Guesses, and Create as they go!"– Provided by publisher.
Identifiers: LCCN 2022039910 | ISBN 9781668920350 (paperback) | ISBN 9781668919330 (hardcover) | ISBN 9781668923016 (pdf) | ISBN 9781668921685 (ebook)
Subjects: LCSH: Body image–Juvenile literature.
Classification: LCC BF724.3.B55 H55 2023 | DDC 155.2–dc23/eng/20220921
LC record available at https://lccn.loc.gov/2022039910

Cherry Lake Publishing would like to acknowledge the work of the Partnership for 21st Century Learning, a network of Battelle for Kids. Please visit *http://www.battelleforkids.org/networks/p21* for more information.

Printed in the United States of America
Corporate Graphics

CHERRY LAKE PRESS

CONTENTS

LET'S TALK ABOUT BODY IMAGE

Body image is how people think and feel about their bodies.

Having a healthy body image means thinking good thoughts about your body. It means feeling **confident** and knowing your body is great just the way it is.

Bodies all look different, and that's okay. Some bodies are bigger, and some are smaller. Some bodies are darker, and some are lighter. Some

Having a positive body image leads to having higher self-esteem. All bodies are different, and everyone can feel good about their body!

bodies are taller, and some are shorter. Some bodies have one kind of hair, and some have another kind. All bodies are beautiful.

There are many reasons bodies can look different. One reason is that people have different **genes**. Genes are like tiny codes inside of you that tell your body what to look like.

Different genes mean that people can have all different kinds of hair textures. All textures are good!

Look!

Look at all of these different strong bodies. What kinds of things are they doing to feel strong?

People with any kind of body can have a healthy body image. There are many ways to have a strong and healthy body. Sometimes what is most healthy for each person can be different. Your body is most healthy when you find ways to feel strong and good. Everyone can find ways to feel this way.

Sometimes people can change things about their bodies. For example, they can change their hair with a haircut or hair color. They can change their ears with

Ask Questions!

Find a grown-up to talk with you about body image. How did they feel about their body when they were a kid? Talk about how you feel about your body if you would like.

piercings. Sometimes people can't change things about their bodies. No one should make someone feel like they have to change their body.

On TV, in movies, in books, and on the internet, bodies can sometimes look perfect. A lot of that is pretend. People make art choices or use photo tricks to make bodies look certain ways.

KIDS AND BODY IMAGE

Body image is important. Everyone deserves to feel good about their bodies and in their bodies.

Sometimes you may hear or see things that make it seem like one kind of body is the best. That's not true. It may seem like people with certain genders need to look a certain way. That's not true either.

Any person can look any kind of way. No one should say anything mean about someone else's body.

Make a Guess!

What would the world be like if everyone felt good about their bodies? What would it feel like?

Having a healthy body image does not mean anyone has to look or feel perfect. A healthy body image is when someone feels good and confident when they look at and think about their body.

Kids can do a lot to feel good about their bodies. They can try doing things that make their bodies feel strong. They can speak to themselves kindly.

Taking care of your body helps take care of your mind.

13

They can speak up if they hear someone saying something mean about someone's body. Sometimes when you stand up for someone, you feel good too.

It's important for good friends to stand up for each other. Having good friendships is good for your health!

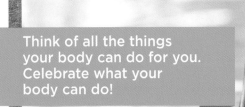
Think of all the things your body can do for you. Celebrate what your body can do!

WHAT'S MOST IMPORTANT TO REMEMBER?

People have different types of bodies. There is no best kind of body. All bodies can be healthy and strong.

Think!

What would you say to someone who said something unkind about someone's body? Who could you ask for help?

Anyone can have a healthy body image if they work at it. There is no such thing as a perfect body or perfect way to look. Healthy bodies are most important.

Healthy bodies are most important.
Any body can be beautiful just as it is.

Confidence in your body image can come from being kind to yourself and doing what you love.

REFLECTING ABOUT BODY IMAGE

How can you feel good about your body? Have you done any of these things before?

What is something you would like the grown-ups at your school to do to help all kids have a healthy body image?

Sometimes people compare their body to other people's bodies. How could comparing bodies make a person feel?

How can you help your body feel healthy and strong?

Create!

Come up with a list of all the things you do to help your body feel good and strong. Draw pictures of what you like to do most.

GLOSSARY

body image (BAH-dee IH-mij) how you see your own body

confident (KAHN-fuh-duhnt) having a strong belief in yourself

genes (JEENZ) part of a cell that determines how you look

healthy (HEL-thee) feeling and being strong and well

photo tricks (FOH-toh triks) ways of making people look better or different in photos

piercings (PEER-sings) holes in a body part for an earring or other decoration

stand up (STAND UHP) defend someone or something

LEARN MORE

Fable Vision: *The Reflection In Me* by Marc Colagiovanni (2017, ~3:30 mins) https://www.youtube.com/watch?v=D9OOXCu5XMg

Book: *Her Body Can* by Katie Crenshaw and Ady Meschke https://www.bodycanbooks.com

Book: *Some Bodies* by Sophie Kennen https://cherrylakepublishing.com/shop/show/53232

Video: lesson preview, lesson available on teacherspayteachers.com Positive Body Image for Kids: Lesson Preview, (2019, ~2 mins) https://www.youtube.com/watch?v=8GfTtqSAz8s

INDEX

ABOUT THE AUTHORS

AnneMarie K. McClain is an educator, researcher, and parent. Her work is about how kids and families can feel good about who they are. She especially loves finding ways to help kids and families feel seen in TV and books.

Lacey J. Hilliard is a college professor, researcher, and parent. Her work is in understanding how grown-ups talk to children about the world around them. She particularly likes hearing what kids have to say about things.